For Elaine

Contents

I

THE NEW EGYPT

I think of my father who believes
a Jew can outwit fate by owning land.
Slave to property now, I mow
and mow, my destiny the new Egypt.
From his father, the tailor, he learned not
to rent but to own; to borrow to buy.
To conform, I disguise myself and drag
the mower into the drive, where I ponder
the silky oil, the plastic casing, the choke.
From my father, I learned the dignity
of exile and the fire of acquisition,
not to live in places lightly, but to plant
the self like an orange tree in the desert
and irrigate, irrigate, irrigate.

Is she also Jewish?

HOLY CARD

We believed the Mosaic injunction against
the graven image, we turned from the forbidden,
attractive man ferrying the toddler across the river,
we rid ourselves of desire for his comforting
hairy arm, his sandaled feet, the kind
gaze softened by dark hair and beard.
We refused St. Christopher along with St. Jerome,
the keys and miniature houses, their reclining lions,
their implausible miracles, their unhappy personal
and professional lives. We trained ourselves not
to want *eternal life in Jesus who loves the little children.*
We knew children like you
and your brothers and sisters,
forced to pray, on car trips, to the patron
saint of travelers. Framed above your beds,
a heart your mother placed, bright red.
Blue fabric, pulled aside, revealed its slippery
materiality like a fleshy genital,
a private part others did not expose.
Every day, the dangers of collision, of fire,
of explosion, of falls and bruises swept
those who skipped confession or mass,
but you—clothed in the invisible
protection the rosary summoned
bead by bead—fell clear of machinery.
The calendar with tiny doors burgeoned
with holy days; gift-wrapped relics and statuettes
arrived in hundreds of households.
Today I hold the laminated card

with the push-out medallion you gave me
for safe travel to New England and think
of the Jewish child fascinated by the saint
torn apart limb from limb, embarrassed by the plastic
swoon of the martyr on the dashboard.
And now, God's commission to St. Christopher
requires this computer-enhanced hologram
of Amtrak plying the northeast corridor,
where a handsome man in a toga walks
the pixilated clouds, sporting a child on his shoulder.

INTERSEX

Because there's a word, there's a way to wonder
if any of our group shagging baseballs
all spring might not have been a girl at all
but a hybrid cultivar. Micki and Jackie
resembled twin ponies, palomino
manes like vanilla frosting. Ruddy turnstones,
Sal and Les tumbled through the neighborhood,
grandstanding for screams. We all wanted to be
boys then, to serve the power we knew
found delight in our swinging from trees.
We wanted to serve the one god of joy
in the body and wreck ourselves at the altar
of summer nights on the city stoop, our shaped parts
sprouting overnight as we slept, changelings.
Sometimes I chose the hard singularity
of the young liege, honor-bound even in defeat.
To the armor and scabbard I cleaved,
make-believe punishments a drubbing I took
to prove my manliness, my worthiness.
Sometimes I starred in my own
midsummer count and dreamed myself
a handsome specimen in bright plumage,
recognizable on the wing, most numerous
in early June when my kind crossed natural barriers.

[handwritten note in margin: This poem's easier to follow. Tomboys]

THE POCONOS

My mother joined *[handwritten: Can you do that?]*
the Leni Lenape

when Pennsylvania Power and Light
dammed

Lake Wallenpaupack
and she turned

eight. In Philadelphia
Bubbe sewed name tags

into underwear and chose
Camp Pine Forest

for its strict counselors
and Friday night corn roasts.

My mother and her sister rose
high into the Poconos,

past waterfalls and rivers,
where the eldest

became an Iroquois
among unruly bunkmates,

raiding the Shawnee
and short-sheeting the Minisink.

My mother fished
peaceably for perch and shad

with the other Leni Lenape
and pursued the arts

and crafts of clay, wood.
She gave her birch bark box

in friendship
and taught the Seneca to build

a gabled frame from saplings.
For seven summers

she portaged and rowed,
roaming the woods with her clan,

and in time,
after Color War,

the tribe made her a Pine Tree—
and she sat at tribal council,

where she presided
over her children,

distinguished
by her compassionate nature,

bartering her freedom
for a modest home on a small tract of land.

I don't really get how
these couplets lend
anything to the poem . . .

MANIFEST DESTINIES

from *The Journals of Lewis and Clark*
—edited by Bernard DeVoto

The ravages of the Small Pox
has reduced this nation not exceeding 300 men
and left them to the insults of their weaker neighbors
which before was glad to be on friendly terms with them

Early this morning the principal Chief
of the lower Village of the Mandans came Down
He packed about 100 lb of fine meat
on his squaw for us
The river is full of floating ice
Presents of Curious Handkerchiefs
arm bands & paint with a twist
of tobacco, medals and flags

Lewis took 15 men and went out
joined the Indians who were at that time
killing the Buffalo on Horseback
One cow was killed on the ice
They drew her out of a vacancy in which she had fallen
and butchered her at the fort
Those we did not get in was taken by Indians
under a Custom which is established among them
Any person seeing a buffalo lying with an arrow
sticking in him takes possession

The wind hard all day from the N.E. & East
Great numbers of Buffalo Swimming the river
I observe near all large gangs of Buffalo wolves

And when the Buffalo move those animals follow
and feed on those killed by accident or those
too poor or fat to keep up with the gang

The beating punishment of one of our men
this day alarmed the Indian Chief very much
When He cried aloud I explained the Cause
of the punishment and the necessity of it
His nation never whipped even their children from birth

I am told that when the Small Pox malady was among them
they Carried their frenzy to extraordinary length
They put their wives & children to death
with a view of their all going together
to some better Country

AUGUST

His legs thicken, harden

He recalls the sap
fueling his limbs

How he loved the cold
challenges of winter
the car skating on ice

Now he looks down
at tight pillars
their pink fissures

He touches his thigh
says *The fluid has risen
above the knee*

I watch him
become tree, then chair

MAN OF THE YEAR

My father tells the story of his life

and he repeats *The most important thing*:
     to love your work.
I always loved my work. I was a lucky man.

This man who makes up half of who I am,
     this blusterer
who tricked the rich, outsmarting smarter men,

gave up his Army life insurance plan
     (not thinking of the future
wife and kids) and brokered deals with two-faced

rats who disappeared his cash but later overpaid
     for building sites.
In every tale my father plays outlaw, a Robin Hood

for whom I'm named, a type of yeoman
     refused admission
into certain clubs. For years he joined no guild—

no *Drapers, Goldsmiths, Skinners, Merchant*
     Tailors, Salters, Vintners—
but lived on prescience and cleverness.

He was the self-inventing Polish immigrant's
     son, transformed
by American tools into Errol Flynn.

As he speaks, I remember the phone calls
        during meals—
an old woman dead in apartment two-twelve

or burst pipes and water flooding rooms.
        Hatless,
he left the house and my mother's face

assumed the permanent worry she wore,
        forced to watch him
gamble the future of the semi-detached house,

our college funds, and his weekly payroll.
        Manorial halls
of Philadelphia his Nottingham,

my father fashioned his fraternity
        without patronage
or royal charters but a mercantile

swagger, finding his Little John, Tinker,
        and Allen-a-Dale.
Wholesalers, retailers, in time they resembled

the men they set themselves against.
        Each year they roast and toast
one member, a remnant of the Grocer's Feast

held on St. Anthony's Day, when brothers
        communed and dined
on swan, capon, partridges, and wine.

They commission a coat of arms, a song,
        and honor my father—
exemplary, self-made, without debt—

as Man of the Year, a title he reveres
        for the distinguished
peerage he joins, the lineage of merry men.

AGAINST PLEASURE

Worry stole the kayaks and soured the milk.
Now, it's jellyfish for the rest of the summer
and the ozone layer full of holes.
Worry beats me to the phone.
Worry beats me to the kitchen,
and all the food is sorry. Worry calcifies
my ears against music; it stoppers my nose
against barbecue. All films end badly.
Paintings taunt with their smug convictions.
In the dark, Worry wraps her long legs
around me, promises to be mine forever.

Thugs hijacked all the good parking spaces.
There's never a good time for lunch.
And why, my mother asks, *must you track*
beach sand into the apartment?
No, don't bother with books,
not reading much these days.
And who wants to walk the boardwalk anyway,
with scam artists who steal your home and savings?
Watch out for talk that sounds too good to be true.
You, she says pointing at me,
don't worry so much.

A PASTURE OF MY PALM

Trembling, desirous, above the display
case, I hovered with my child's hand. Beneath,
porcelain palominos stamped their feet,
and foals stood with their long legs splayed. I longed

to take one home, to place it on a shelf
and study the raised leg, the frothy mane.
Then, cupping the horse's shape in my hand,
I'd make a pasture of my palm, a field.

No one was looking, no one, I reasoned,
would know I'd swiped it, toy in my pocket.
That night I stroked the caramel china.
I was galloping, when my mother walked

into my room. She knew I was lying.
(*The horse? a gift . . .*) I cried when she told me
we'd speak with the manager the next day.
In his office I stood, wept, but even

then I was really crying for the cheap
horse back in the glass case, my mother,
my foolish and punishable desires,
the future taking shape: corral, stampede.

hyperbole... become
a huge statement

SOUND VIEW

Like driftwood,
antlered,
    a deer
foams toward shore.

    The size of the hull
determines the drag,
    and the living mast
displaces the air,

    storms its greasy shingles
from sea nettle,
    snorts the salt
from its black fist

    of a snout.
A container ship
    menaces the horizon
with its calculus

    of cubic feet and knots.
Meditation point,
    the tanker resists
my efforts at composure.

    When I close my eyes
the bright boxes
    mother explosives
the way the pastoral

    turns elegy,
transfiguring the bodies in its path.

[handwritten annotation: Invasion of the industrial in nature]

SALON

Acolyte at the font, my mother
bends before basin and hose
where Jackie soaps her fine head,
adjusting pressure and temperature.
How many times has she
bared her throat, her clavicle,
beside the other old women?
How many times the regular
cleansing and surrender to the cold chair,
the sink, the detergents, the lights,
the slick of water down the nape?
Turbaned and ready,
she forgoes the tray of sliced bagels
and donuts, a small, private dignity.

Vivienne, the manicurist, dispels despair,
takes my mother's old hands into her swift
hands and soaks them to soften
the cuticles before the rounding and shaping.
As they talk my mother attends
to the lifelong business of revealing
and withholding, careful to frame each story
while Vivienne lacquers each nail
and then inspects each slender finger,
rubbing my mother's hands
with the fragrant, thin lotion,
each summarizing her week, each
condemning that which must be condemned,
each celebrating the manicure and the tip.

Sometimes in pain, sometimes broken
with grief in the parking lot,
my mother keeps her Friday appointment
time protected now by ritual and tradition.

The fine cotton of Michael's white shirt
brushes against her cheek as they stare
into the mirror at one another.
Ennobled by his gaze, she accepts
her diminishment, she who knows herself
his favorite. In their cryptic language
they confide and converse, his hands busy
in her hair, her hands quiet in her lap.
Barrel-chested, Italian, a lover of opera,
he husbands his money and his lover, Ethan;
only with him may she discuss my lover and me,
and in this way intimacy takes the shape
of the afternoon she passes in the salon,
in the domain of perfect affection.

Non-judging

what is perfect affection?

what is a
mangle?

In the history of domestic objects, a good design
inspires innovation, miniaturization, a female
character such as Ann, Duchess of Hamilton,
who ordered a mangle from Edinburgh,
1696, leading to the improved
mangle patented in England, 1774.

After that it was Blue Monday, reverse rotary washers,
the steam-heated mangle, the spring clothespin,
the Shaker elder, 1869, with his centrifugal
dryer, and the famous Americans—Hotpoint, Maytag,
Speed Queen—beginning their litanies.
Like a new foal, the ironing board stood upright.

When Chicago's washerwomen left
to work the farms, Mary Livermore borrowed machines
for the first cooperative laundry—
1862—and fifty women rolled up their sleeves.
Tenements of housedresses, overalls, tablecloths,
and curtains rose, supervised by Livermore, critic of the isolated

household, critic of the schools where immigrant girls,
five years old, learned to operate miniature
washbasins and mangles. *Home making . . .
is a sweated industry*, said Ethel Howes, who favored
socialized housework, community kitchens,
a bridge from private to public. Today

you find the mangle housed in a corner
with the washboard, basin, and wringer.
And to the laundress,
maid, cook, nurse, and seamstress:
take the stay-press from the machine,
it's casual Friday, it's wash-and-wear, it's wrinkle-free.

THE DRAWER

Let the stapler lie next to the field guide. So what
if, feeling around, you find your old laminated license? Slotted supports
may work for some people, but for you, the sun

brightening the corner with the passport says it all: you're a joyful
mess of a housekeeper, discovering the transistor radio,
the scissors, a bathing suit, nothing in full view

of the worker. Who doesn't love a sliding tray? Partitions
for pie tins, pot lids, and cookie sheets? *The family silver*
is easy to find when all spoons are in one slot.

A drawer of this type can be lined with tarnish-proof fabric
if desired. In Somerville, years ago, floral shelf paper turned
gray, then brown. You'd swipe it with a sponge, humming

We gotta get outta this place. Batteries. Tampons. Songbooks
from the '60s. The miscellaneous and the mismatched.
The scratched. The damaged. Many came and went

from that communal household, where labeled
cardboard boxes took on a sour smell. But someone
knew to store flour in a can; somebody's lover

built tip-out bins for Brillo and sponge. A few worked
at the co-op, you were a grad student, and all you owned
fit into the dresser from Brighton. It would be years

before you came to appreciate the proper height of a chopping
block, a well-made spice rack, a vertical file for dishes.
Even now, a braided lanyard from camp counselor days

spirals from the drawer, beneath photos of the woman
you love and a vial of sacred dirt from the church in Chimayo—
collected the summer you traveled with nothing but a backpack.

THE DOME FIRE

Flames crown the ponderosa pines
    torching tree after dry tree
From the air a jeweled tiara of fire
    spurts between sleeves of smoke
    seething north and west

Seventeen thousand acres
    burn in the Jemez Mountains
circling the Stone Lions shrine
    and the trails we hiked
    in the long decades of friendship

All of our beautiful places are burning
    you said *the Painted Cave and field house*
the cavates carved into volcanic cliffs
    with their corncobs and doorway latillas
    the brush in Capulin and Alamo canyons

Burning near Los Alamos
    where they buried tritium and plutonium
with a half-life of 76 million years
    burning so close you imagine packing
    your children and leaving the state

Smoke stings your eyes in Santa Fe
    as they dig the fuel break by hand
establishing a line around the fire
    Already hot by late April you said
    No rain for a year

A decade ago I rode through Yellowstone
    blackened the guide said *when inrushing*
winds from all sides fed the fire
    On the forest floor gold and sapphire
    wildflowers led us from that scorched place

to a field where we camped and turned our horses
    loose to graze   Green saliva stained their teeth
Rose and turquoise saturated mountain phlox
    and larkspur   *It begins with the wildflowers*
    she said *and then the world comes back*

[handwritten marginalia: Poem ends on a hopeful note beginning w/ mention of wildflowers]

You are the spirit
                    of this place—
each shingled gable
            each pine-planked   room
                single bed and crook-necked lamp.
                                Oak table.   I touch the chenille
                                            bedspread
                                        rescued from the wreckage of Queens,
                        the faded India-print throw . . .
            Who doesn't remember the swirling
                    designs for sale   in every shop   in Central Square, 1969?

You've hung the cast-iron pots
                            set out the flashlights and bug spray
                                    arranged the geological survey maps
                that we might be Bat Mitzvah girls
                                        grown and hiking up Monadnock
For the children
                    a giant rope swing
                                    above the mowing
and a drawer filled with spangles   and scissors   and glue
            An industrious mess pleases you
who loves the order   of wicker chair and bookcase
                    woodstove and bench

You are the spirit
                    of this cabin with a footed bathtub
            an old Webster's   doors studded
                    with black latches   we lift and drop
            for the satisfying music

[handwritten margin note: I like the mention of an old Webster's — they're the doors — so similar!]

26

We could be   our grandmothers
in a Ukrainian hermitage   The pogroms are still
years away
Not rifles but rucksacks stream
through the woods—
See how your hand invites
the imagination inside to feed?
It's the long weekend   of white tail and woodpecker
We don't have to put on our good clothes 'til Tuesday

I don't quite see the connection to design here — is it to parallel 'architecture' in the title?

studies the estuary
sings to the knobbed and channeled whelks
pauses over strings of circular egg cases
tenants the cartilaginous skate and next spring's stinging sea nettle
as well as the fishing boats that depart and return in February darkness
setting out in optimism for that is a requirement of those who fish
and tying up in envy, for that is also a requirement

after the snowstorm, the bay
turns from the snow-covered industry of New London
rocks in her dark enclosure and reveals her runic alphabet
knows the Gulf Stream and the osprey will return in time
considers the theory that water retains memory and is therefore
a kind of living mind, similar in spirit to the souls
of the haiku poets of Japan and the Chinese watercolorists

after the snowstorm, the bay overrides the causeway
where a plashy convergence of waters salts the freshets
pickles a chassis with briny pocks, dismisses the retaining wall
and strikes with a shower of spray the raised roadbed
illustrates that chief among the disciplines is the study
of optics, for the gull will know a gar
and the kingfisher dive headfirst to earn her belt and crest

after the snowstorm, the bay hosts the red-breasted mergansers
lighthearted on the breakers but growing moody by March
welcomes the Brotherhood of the Order of the Blue Heron
fancies the brown pelican with fetching currents and tides
but fails to lure the large bird from warmer waters
glows at night with the comb jellies that emit their own light and prove
the sky of stars is not superior to the bay of fire

really cool attention to sound here

confusing

I REALLY MISS PUNCTUATION.

BORDERLINE

in memory of Jill Wendy Becker, 1954–1987

Brink, brow, verge, brim. I grew
adjacent and then away—leaving you, sister,

on the margin of error, your uncultivated strip,
staring at coastlines where others converged.

Not for you the adaptation, the going along, the realistic
expectation, the rules regarding performance

in work or the timbre of friendship. Not for you
a rowboat with oars and oarlocks from which to paddle

to mudflats and there encounter the stargazer
that buries itself in the muddy sand

or the common shipworm that opens wood
and confounds the shipwright's carpentry.

Oh, the co-housing arrangements of bivalves!
How they drill and devour each other,

like us on the biochemical ledges
where your doctor knew no drug or medication

to help fifteen years ago. You lived between
diagnoses, your illness nonspecific, placeless,

and occupied your indeterminacy
not as protective coloration but condition,

today characterized by some as trauma
in early development affecting brain function

or an intrauterine factor
to which you were genetically predisposed.

Certain patterns, some studies show,
of overinvolvement between parent and child

may be causative factors. You tenanted
an invalidating space where sandbars rose

and disappeared overnight, where organisms
are fragile and prone to rapid deterioration;

thus, mind and place co-create each other
over time, and in you, magical thinker, impulsive

brooder, both remained lawless,
mutable, labile. Neither barrier beach

nor tide pool nor undersea meadow
could nourish you, as the rank estuary sustains

the bottom-dwelling searobin
that learns to walk on wing-shaped fins.

II

ANGEL SUPPORTING ST. SEBASTIAN

Shot with arrows and left for dead,
against the angel's leg, Sebastian sinks.
In time, he'll become the patron

saint of athletes and bookbinders. ← funny juxtaposition
But for now, who wouldn't want to be
delivered into the sculpted arms

of this seraph, his heavenly
shoulders and biceps?
The artist understood the swoon

of doctrine, its fundamental
musculature, and the human need
to lean against the lusty form,

accept the discourse that assigns
to each of us a winged guardian
whispering into our ringing ears.

This one's actually coherent; that's nice.

SOOT AND SPIT

How may I know you, James Castle? In the photo,
wearing farm worker's denim, you are a man
holding a hat at your side. The visible tree is leafless.
You have dark hair, a broad face. I would not guess
that you don't write or read. Or speak.

Or that for ink you mixed soot from a wood-burning
stove with saliva and drew with sharpened sticks.
On envelopes and packaging. On flattened matchboxes.
Sometimes adding string and paste to make constructions
or small books of colored pulp. Undated. Untitled.

I invent boarding school despots who flog your refusals.
I invent your withdrawal to homemade
technologies, to fabricate the inner life of the stable and inhabit
a place of such tenderness we cannot misunderstand
the scratched walls, the framed stalls, the pitch of open roofing

and darkness gathering on your unembellished grain bins.
In such a space I dream of barn owls flying
and nesting and turning their ancient faces in welcome,
for I have come into your Idaho—a condition without
distraction or sound, irony or compromise—to find you,

but how may I know you, James Castle?
By the shadows that hide the animals and filigree the lathing?
In the shed with its floor of packed dirt, dust ornaments
open shelves of preserves, and someone beyond
the picture plane draws in silence, beloved, at home.

QUALITIES BOYS LIKE BEST IN GIRLS

from *Guide for Today's Home Living*
—Mildred Andrews and Hazel Hatcher

Boys like a girl who is alert, full of life and fun to be with.
She doesn't sit on the sidelines and expect to be entertained.

A girl who shows friendliness and interest in others attracts boys.
They like a girl who overlooks their faults and makes them feel
at ease in embarrassing situations.

A girl's appearance is important to boys. A pretty girl catches
the eye. Poise, good posture, a sunny disposition, and a fresh
well-groomed look are characteristics boys admire.

Hoping to make a more pleasing appearance by using cosmetics,
a girl needs to know how to wear make-up
without its being overdone or obvious.

Punctuality is a trait that makes a hit with boys.
A self-conscious boy is apt to feel ill-at-ease if he has to spend
too long a time conversing with the girl's parents.

Boys like a girl who is sincere. A girl
who is straightforward appeals to boys.

Boys dislike a girl who tries to make an impression
by prattling on about how much things cost.

Boys place a high value on loyalty, too.

Boys prefer a girl who shows some intelligence—
who knows when to laugh and when to be serious,
when to talk and when to listen.

Boys like a girl who is modest about her accomplishments.
They feel insecure when a girl gives the impression
that she is mentally superior to them.

This is a really pointed
poem and I don't
like how telly it
is. But that's the
point.

SIMPLE DARK

Barn doors open at each end—
        inside, animal stink,
                wood shavings, broadax,

nakedness in the hayloft.
        To fall in
                with the simple dark,

to finger the wooden hinge,
        lock, hook, abraded stalls:
                this feeling your way

in the barn a first
        knowledge, where thought roams,
                a barn cat.

Dreaming, you clip
        lead shank to halter and groom
                in the drowse

of a standing horse
        whose legs frame
                a passageway of light.

You're drawn to thresholds
        and overhangs, corridors
                of segmented, dark sequences,

cross-hatching and thatch.
        An outbuilding shadows
                a figure walking to town

on a brown wash.

  Touchstone of summer days.

   In the village,

a cooper makes

  of oak staved casks,

   her barn doors open at each end.

Uh, this crashes.
It's inside-out.

ORIENTEER:

THE CHILDHOOD DRAWINGS OF

WILLIAM STEEPLE DAVIS, 1884–1961

Orient, New York

Prologue

Forty years after his death,
I lived in his house for a year. His drawings mapped
the drafty windows of the studio, where I found his old paint box
and stared at his view. Imaginary friend,
he oriented my solitude.

♣

Four years old, knees tucked beneath the desk,
William draws the *Sunshine* steamer returning on long swells.
He draws bakery and dairy carts,
horse drawn and hand lettered, and the sole
proprietors clutching reins and whips.
As for the horses, he gets them all wrong—
or right, depending on your reading
of the creatures' rubbery legs and arched feet,
and the bay-salted child's meticulous
rendering of an overturned wagon,
runaway gone, driver airborne.

Blinkered and harnessed, end of the century,
a horse stands hitched to a sleigh
with curving runners. Blizzard of 1888.
On the bay, ice-boaters cheer; scooters slide,
brass blades flashing, punts rigged
with jib and mainsail. From Shelter Island,

Cook and his oxen freight goods over the freeze
        to Greenport—where someone's cutting ice
                to pack with sawdust, salt, and hay.
        And a hundred men with shovels come to free
the packed train rails frozen to Mineola.

        No mail since Saturday. William draws
                King Street, snow blurring dormers and gables.
        Soon, the Douglass' *spite house* disappears.
Indoors, a gun surmounts the mantel, coal brims the hod.
        William pencils a thick grey border around
                the cookstove studded with cast-iron pots
        and teakettle; a stovepipe takes a right turn,
leaves the picture. Below, a wood box bulges.
        Carrie Davis shuttles tureen and chafing dish
                to table, where round loaves and cheese board
        rise to the dining room ceiling.

In his village scenes, the horses' legs—penciled,
        erased, re-penciled—show a struggle with perspective,
                as when William draws the shipbuilder's saw
        (large, articulated teeth hanging from a nail)
or the high-waisted carpenter, reaching
        long arms to sand the watermelon-shaped hull.
                By seven, he knows the distant fishing boats,
        their boxy forward cabins, will meet in collinear lines.
By nine, he seeks the abridged angles of the wagon
        on a slope, harvestmen climbing scratchy hay, until
                the storm dashes boat and wagon with slanted lashes.

At the center of the world, in the studio
on King Street, William studies his paint box
        and toolbox to reproduce with subtle shading
                the dented tubes of oils, their densely lettered labels,
        his palette knives and wooden-handled brushes.
He sketches finials and forged lift-latches,
        the parlour's patterned curtains and cane chairs.
                His panoramas show the cycling craze,
        the church spires, steamboats, skiffs, and smacks
anchoring for barber and cobbler shops
        and the Eastern Telegraph.

                In the fractious harbor, thirty coastermen call
        Orient *home port*, and all know Charlie Davis'
homeschooled Willie, with his pencils and busy
        silence trained on the transport of egg crates and chickens.
                Tiny black-hatted men race across his pictures,
        pushing dollies stacked with bags of cauliflower.
They belong to Orient's extended family
        of oyster packers and hoisters, dockers
                loading scallops, before the new
        century favors the automobile,
foreclosing two hotels and general stores.

        And here, a bearded fellow with topper
                and cane strolls past a plate glass window
        where the shopkeeper adjusts a framed painting—
summer people sailing Long Island Sound—
        signed *William Steeple Davis, 1893.*

SUBJECT / MATTER

> All great artists are in love with subject matter.
> —John Marin

A shadow on the shed—
the tree's great arm—
evokes the homely affection I feel
for the lexicon of reds layered on old barns.
A ghost branch, the penumbra turns
a trick of light, and I'm off listing beauty's dark
properties: shutter atilt, tin roof scored
and pocked, John Marin's *Winter from My Back Window,
Cliffside, New Jersey, 1929*. Not a painting
you'd associate with him, this jumble of rooflines
bristling with snow, low buildings, wooden
sides heaving with heat, cold, energy, his palette
of gray and brown.

      All year I've watched the country
contract, expand, break apart, stratocumulus:
on the stained-glass surf of Long Island,
on Sixth Avenue with my love, in the turn-of-the-century
Village splintering, vertical; at Pier 40, percussive
gale hammering where the Hudson dips and twists,
into the city's divisible canyons, my fist a star
around the cold apartment keys. All year love
makes of me the modernist who could not sleep,
who joined the Cubist revolution
after the Salon of 1908, and broke
from himself, and returned to North America
on *a written sea* of bone, glass, metal, paint.

THE MINIATURISTS

in memory of painter Donald Evans, 1945–1977

When she showed me the canceled stamps
    of Evans' imaginary
countries, their carved postmarks,

I thought how lovely to live in a nation
    he named *Stein*,
where, to celebrate the fiftieth anniversary

of *Tender Buttons*, the post office
    issued
stamps with quotations from the text.

She lauded his studies of pears, his love
    of appearances,
his taxonomies of seashells and palm trees

and took me, first, to fictitious *Nadorp*
    for the children's series,
stamps of paired objects, elusive meanings:

bow tie & rabbit; sunrise & comma. Whatever
    he loved, he loved
to scale, and then scaled down: an archipelago

of Friends and Lovers (*Amis et Amants*),
    or the state
named for the artist *Weisbecker*, in whose loft

he painted the homely *National Chair Works*—
      four chairs
in praise of Lower East Side hospitality.

She embraced her own treasures: World War I
      memorabilia, vintage lesbian
pulp fiction, insects in amber, recordings of Caruso.

Preserved like the cat mummy in the British Museum,
      the complete handwritten draft
of her dissertation stood in its portable sanctuary.

She'd take it from the tabernacle, part the silk wrapper,
      and show me the inscrutable
cross-hatchings, pages smelling of lemonwood.

Over dinner, we enjoyed watercolors of *Mangiare*,
      for which he named cities
after Italian dishes and created the region called *Pasta*,

composed of twenty-five provinces, commemorated
      on festive stamps
to philatelic standards, properly perforated.

When the affair ended, I walked each day
      to the tiny park
with the diminutive swing set and pumped

my enormous feet against the small sky.

[handwritten marginal note:] really pretty. The end comes so abruptly I'm left to assume the affair did, too. I'm a little unsure what it means.

44

GREAT SLEEPS I HAVE KNOWN

Once in a cradle in Norway folded
like Odin's eight-legged horse Sleipnir
as a ship in full sail transported the dead to Valhalla

Once on a mountain in Taos after making love
in my thirties the decade of turquoise and silver

After your brother walked into the Atlantic
to scatter your mother's ashes his khakis soaked
to the knees his shirtsleeves blowing

At the top of the cottage in a thunderstorm
once or twice each summer covetous of my solitude

Immediately following lunch
against circadian rhythms, once
in a bunk bed in a dormitory in the White Mountains

Once in a hollow tree in Wyoming
A snow squall blew in the guide said *tie up your horses*

The last night in the Katmandu guest house
where I saw a bird fly from a monk's mouth
a consolidated sleep of East and West

Once on a horsehair mattress two feet thick
I woke up singing
as in the apocryphal story of my birth
at Temple University Hospital

On the mesa with the burrowing owls
on the mesa with the prairie dogs

Willing to be lucky
I ran the perimeter road in my sleep
Sometimes my dead sister visited my dreams

Once on the beach in New Jersey
after the turtles deposited their eggs
before my parents grew old, nocturnal

SUMMER'S TALE

Isn't the story better embellished?
Aren't we happier wooded and beached,
burnished with patina? Curved, mauved?
Take out the bee sting and emergency room,
the ungracious guest, the rainy weekends.
Aren't we better off trailing lilac streamers?
Pretend we take the Zakim Bridge at sunset,
halyards clank in Hingham harbor as we toast.
Who could choose one god among all the bright
feathers of August or tell a summer story
without its old fishhooks and salt-weathered prospects?
I'll add the foreign stamps, the halogens;
you bring the clambake and watercolors.
Let's give the contractor a bit part in the kayak.

Thats a nice,
affirming poem
It makes me
happy, esp.
because its such
a writers' activity

47

THE DOGS OF SANTORINI

The dogs of Santorini sleep on marble
paving stones in the sun that sucks
the moisture from their tongues and dries
the whitewashed walls to dust

One dreams of naked men carrying fish
and a large woman holding a fishing net
a storeroom with cooking pots and roasting grills
a vat into which a rat's tail disappears

Warriors with ox-hide shields and boar's tusk
helmets rout them   Thirst and bedevilments
of weather torment them   Still the dogs
of Santorini sleep in the general's dooryard

They pity the cats of Rhodes   eaten during wartime
who pity the goats of Naxos   tethered standing for years
and everyone pities the donkeys of Crete
Such sadness in the animal world

The dogs sleep beside bougainvillea
with pink bracts   in clay pots   at the hotel reception
When I fashion a bowl and fill it with water
they trot away   seeking better outcomes

Snouts in the air   the dogs of Santorini smell
the *meltemi* blowing in from Paros and know
the large ships will dock while the small boats will cancel
and we'll be stuck in Oia   waiting for our luck

to change so we can sail the crater
Now rain pelts rock and storms the awning
we hunch beneath   sipping coffee with the beached
sailors mending their nets   fingers like gristle

Asleep in wet spools on marble-paved streets
the dogs of Santorini resemble
grapevines grown ground-level against the winds
adapted to survive in salt and ash

HEAD OF AN OLD MAN

Fire and water god, successor by sword,
shall we save your teeth and nails for amulets

around our necks, or fast and rent our dresses
when we hear the news?

Accompanied this far by your thunder
and drought, your book of shattered laws,

we follow the procession to the grove
where the living learn to mourn the dying god.

Your head is a melon, a helmet, a planet
we'll consult as oracle, preserved.

Now, Gardener King, pass into Paradise,
you who mastered the wild technologies,

who swallowed creation, who returned
to inhabit new doctrines, transmigrant,

now invisible, now taking human form.
What form will you take now, winged charioteer,

who once bathed your father in a porcelain tub?
You feared him for so long you never learned

how to lose him, both of you too foolish, stubborn.

DESCRIPTION

How many words for glisten, sparkle, glister?
　　　How many ways to convey the shimmer
and glitter on the bay, the dazzle of faceted

glass incoming with the tide? A crystalline
　　　vessel of red motion, shape of a kayak, skims
the light-mottled surface; the sailor retrieves

a runaway rowboat, his yellow life vest burning
　　　in the glare. Now he's sitting in the watertight
opening, tying one craft to another, as I am tying

his dappled excursion to my own purposes,
　　　to my pleasure in the reticulated
shapes that dapple the hour. The swells

compose a mosaic I read by analogy:
　　　breaker to anvil, froth to bullion,
crest to shield. Now a Viking story swarms

troughs into helmets, into the fittings
　　　we saw in the Oslo museum,
the delicate ship displayed

like a large animal in a small room, walls scarcely
　　　tall enough for the mast, vessel starting
to drift in its mooring, evoking the dark

harbor where halyards clanked and docks creaked,
　　　the boats so close to one another
we heard the whispers of those who slept on the sea.

51

III

RAIN

I decided to love its drenching monopolies
for it was like this: cartels of imported rain
marined the yard with brackish-water jellies.
Stockholders issued certificates for more rain:
the deck floated off, raft in the lake of the street.
I slept on the sofa, dehumidifying,
while a syndicate somewhere bought large blocks
of securities and sold them in small parcels of rain
to the municipality, now *waterfront property*.
We didn't stand a chance.
My neighbor opened a small café
on the picturesque harbor that used to house his lawn.
In the rain, we drank strong coffee; the ferry sulked.
As I said, I chose to take a positive attitude,
so I put on a striped shirt and danced the isthmus dance.
Rain sank the mainland as we debated our options.
Like Noah's wife I gave up pride of place.
When my lover came home from work, we built
a houseboat with an awning and filled our sails
with a waterproof optimism, hoping to run into a few friends
who'd taken the rain into their own hands and gone pelagic.

MAH-JONGG FANTASIA

With the crack of synthetic bone on bone,
       mother wins with the East Wind drawn from the wall,
          and I'm her Winter Scholar, growing

       bamboo in water, setting out lacquered
bowls of mixed nuts and tiny goldfish for the ancestors.
       Fingering ivory tiles, mother tells the future:

          Even the women from Manila
      will invite her into their game
of deadpan experts old as Confucius.

       Today my mother will be the *Ju*,
          the Chinese character for *one*, the bar
      of a door or a barrier being lifted,

and I'll be the latch rising, the will that draws
       her through the gate, where incense smokes
          to appease husband and sister

       calling her home from the quay.
Plum Blossom in silk, she selects the skiff
       called *Incomplete Set of Seasons*,

          where I, Spring Fisherman,
      net carp and cook chestnuts in ginger root.
Our boat plies the East China Sea,

       as she calligraphs a mountain scene,
          speaking fluent Mandarin,
       explaining a line, a bough,

the one hundred and forty-four tiles
    that pass through her hands, as she becomes
        the Orchid Flower and I her Summer Woodcutter.

MAIL ORDER

Because I had nothing my parents wanted
or could use, I sent them bread—8-grain and 3-seed,
San Francisco sourdough, Jewish rye,

anything bakehouse with peasant crust.
When they tore into a loaf of challah
and reported the saffron-colored braids

just right, I rejoiced like a mother—
not one who gives her breast to her child
but one who trusts her child's care to strangers.

NOW

Now that I have the whole afternoon to myself
I can forget my twenty-five-year plan of living
on the Paros beach with friends as the school year begins.

Now that the rain has moved inland
I can surrender the old Madison Square Garden
dressage dream of perfect balance on a horse's back.

Now that the forecast says clear weather through Friday
I can give up the dream that my parents live to one-hundred-
and-twenty, still driving and doing their own grocery shopping.

Now that I have three hours to spend before I go
to the dump, and leftovers with which to make a chicken sandwich,
I can forego my dream of breeding standard poodles,

though I like to picture many pens with black puppies sprawling
over my groomed lawn, though a handsome poodle
meets me at the door with a glass of white wine.

Now that my neighbor has finished his mowing
I can hear myself think. About death: how it occupies
every living space I can imagine, though I can't hold the thought—

Now that a breeze permits me to understand this day
will not merge with others into a synopsis of the summer,
now that I've gone this far, now that you've come with me,

I can give up my dream of biking from Boston to San Francisco
in a skintight jersey covered with ads, mid-semester, reciting the names
of North American birds and whistling all the way to the Pacific.

OLD DOG

Chose the harbor for its smells—
knotted wrack, sea roach, small gull.
Stumbled then sank where she could
feel the breeze smack her ears, flanks.
Admiring, I watched her bed
the sand, paw cracked shells, let go
the rest. Walking home, she ate
something rank. Then stank. Then slept,
deaf to the mailman, his steps,
deaf to letters clattering
through the slot. I wrote and read.
She woke to scratch and fix her
gaze on me. Sat before the
metal bowl I filled for her.

ISLAND OF DAILY LIFE

in memory of Sandra Kanter, 1944–2004

This one is for Sandy
    who loves poems about ordinary things.
        For her, I'll keep my abstractions

    to a minimum and praise
the open carpentry of the summer cabins
    for their impromptu shelves

        where every ledge invites a wildflower bouquet
    or a drawing from a child at camp
or a special stone plucked from the lake,

    and I praise the lake
        with its dappled beach and sloping light,
    the comforting iterations

of rowboat, bathing cap, splash,
    where lakefront trees and small docks
        flare in the late afternoon, and a neighbor

    calls softly to her daughter *it's time
to go, don't forget your things* . . .
    This poem gets up early for the Saturday

        yard sale and celebrates the evening
    walk across the mowing
through low-bush blueberries.

Sometimes guests from the city.
        Always the dog in his summer
haircut announcing his arrival.

This poem honors the poached fish and the beans,
      the goat cheese and the wine,
          the poems read aloud after dinner

    for their attention
to the quiddities, to aspects
   of our communal selves

        sheared of the theoretical.
   This poem celebrates the passing
of the dish and the return of the bowl,

    the full moon now high
        above October lakes, shining
on a thousand forgotten beach books.

HEAD OF AN ANGEL

I've given up trying to decide
what Dürer intended and accept myself
for what I am—androgynous, sublime.

Staminate and pistillate, my flower's
immortal, and maybe that's the point
of the artist's invitation to look

at the stem of my sinuous neck,
the grey ink and white heightening
he brushed on my imperishable curls.

What I'm listening for, Venetian blue,
you infer from my upturned eyes, my mind
through which the mind of God is passing.

COHORT

We've spilled onto the wooden steps and put
our best faces forward for the photograph.
Early fall, we don't know one another yet,
can't see the friendships that will form and who
will fall into her work as into rapture.
We've spilled onto the wooden steps and let
the flat morning light hit each composed mouth
and cheek, each cardigan, each cotton blouse.
This is the first occasion of the year.
Some faces ask *what am I doing here?*

THE OUTSIDE AGITATOR

The outside agitator remembers
my blue knapsack on the floor of the student union,
my hand raised, lonely, in the air.

For weeks I dipped brush into paste,
fixed posters on poles, because I loved her
helmet of hair and heavy orange work boots.

I remember her sadness—like a pamphlet
stuffed in the bottom of a book bag, something
I kept feeling for—

and her urging that I drop out
of college to make the revolution.
On the Boston Common, unable to choose one

banner, I nipped like a rogue sheepdog
at the fraying groups. Then returned to class.
Now, in a dream, the outside agitator

knocks on the door of my dorm room,
her hair the bronze of late summer grass.
She promises we will make love

in the back of her Saab after my Yeats seminar.
Forget your classes, she urges.
Outside, the sisters-at-arms converge

to march for human rights, against the war.
I face their banners and cries for justice,
their bodies on the line.

AUTUMN MEASURE

Violence done to the body
to save the body: tomorrow
my friend will leave the hospital
without her breasts. We say *at least*
she has her life, her work, her legs.
Fate's impersonal face looks back
at me from every burning bush.
The crack I hear isn't a bullet
but another apple falling
hard on the tin roof overhead.

LODGING

What did I tell myself about
those early November days suddenly
bright with August heat? That we lay
on the ground, morning sun
on our faces; that joy blossomed
inside me like lavender dahlias.

Walking the dog, I mentioned the corn
beginning to fall. You gave me
the word for it—*lodging*—
and bent to cradle the stalk, the ear,
explaining how farmers let plants
stand and dry out before harvest.

Like the curb chain closing
the horse's mouth against the bit,
the season pressed against us.
The corn, lodging in rows, had to come down.
Against your burnished arm
and your flushed cheek, I took my place.

LATE BUTCH-FEMME

Long accustomed to playing the butch
I saw you for the femme I thought you were—
long waisted, well bred, the hostess who knew
to fold the napkin in the wineglass. But I had not
watched you square your shoulders before the arborist,
determined to take down the holly to save the oak.

No, you said, *the pin oak goes, the holly stays.*
The gutter man who wants his check will have
to repair the drain he botched. *Please have your son
call me,* you say, your fingers ready for another call.
In the cellar, among the foraged dressers, you measure
and sand and strip. Come up for the lunch I made you,
O handy lover, with your retractable blade,
your small drill, your paint brushes bristling.

BIRDS OF PREY

The cream breast of the hawk glides overhead.   *a*
Titmice scatter seeds by the coal bin.   *b*
O lay me down in the sleep of the dead.   *a*
In Pennsylvania hills, developers steal in.   *b*

Titmice scatter seeds by the coal bin.   *a*
We skied to a field where new houses rose.   *b*
In Pennsylvania hills, developers steal in;   *a*
on rural roads the farms foreclose.   *b*

We skied to a field where new houses rose
on the phantom fencerow where creatures hid.
Along rural roads the farms foreclose,
and land goes for the highest bid.

On the phantom fencerow where creatures hid
you cursed the bulldozer and the company men.
Where land goes for the highest bid
you count bear and deer among your kin.

You cursed the bulldozer and the company men.
An owl hoots to her mate across the pines.
You count bear and deer among your kin.
The great horned ignores all boundary lines.

An owl hoots to her mate across the pines.
You split your wood and stack it by the shed.
The great horned ignores all boundary lines
and claims the winter sky instead.

You split your wood and stack it by the shed,
pine-tar the skis and leave them on the porch.
The owl takes a crow, leaves feathers where it bled.
The cream breast of the hawk flies overhead.

Violence of
the image
underscores
the developers

OK, TUCKER

You win. My arm got tired of throwing the ball
before you got tired of scrambling up the river-
bank to fetch it. OK, Tucker, you can come, too.
Since you open the door with your clever snout
I'm not about to shove you back in. You win
the beauty contest, the most finicky eater award,
and the like-a-dog-with-a-bone prize; you win
the first-one-in-the-car sweepstakes. Look,
Tucker, we had no choice when we squared off
in your adolescence, we had to get along, it was a live-
and-let-live situation, both of us in love with her.
OK, I bribed you with biscuits and rides;
you conned me with a handshake and a smile.
Remember hide-and-seek in the cornfield,
the jack-in-the pulpit, the lady slipper?
That week at the beach with smelly gulls
wrapped in slime and tangled lines of seaweed?
And a pen of chickens? You had it made, but no!
Old girl, you chased the phantom squirrel
up the slope again and again, returned
slack-jawed, refused to come off the porch,
stood your ground in freezing November rain,
showed your dog's teeth when I showed my human
fear and for good measure ran circles around me—
when I was her woman, but you were her dog.

ON FRIENDSHIP

after Horace

Come down, M, stop sulking in that tree.
If the contractor came late and the workers shingling the barn
made a mistake, if the fuel tank in the truck's kaput, if your dead
friend's dog won't eat dinner,
pluck a few raspberries from the October garden.
OK, so you have to dig up the dahlias!

Still holding a grudge about that trip to Italy? Our bad sex life
after our good sex life? (Darling, must we return to the Tigris and Euphrates?)
After twenty years of friendship, we're still lousy
at talking to each other, two middle-aged women
in an age of non-potable water on Long Island,
lethal viruses housed offshore, the scallop harvest at record lows.

Let me recommend Horace, who combined passion with a practical love
for the snafu, who accepted the bungler, the perfectionist, the one
who must have a pear-shaped glass with a narrow top
for aromatic liquors, the two-faced, the evasive, the worried.
He knew that friendship is neither intermittent, nor divisible
into parts, but aboriginal, discordant, the new music.

M, come down from that tree and listen to the apples
dropping on the tin roof. We've been friends since the cradle
of civilization, a pair of foragers watching the deer at midnight
sustain themselves on the rotten, the fallen.

[handwritten marginal note, with a brace pointing to the lines beginning "He knew that friendship is neither intermittent..."] a representation of human nature that is neither idealistic, nor condemning.

72

WITH TWO CAMELS AND ONE DONKEY

Art does not reproduce the visible, it makes visible.
—Paul Klee

May we walk into our lives as into a watercolor,
grounded in sunlight, with two large ruminants and a baying ass.
May we go by foot, hot paving stones giving way to the Perfume Makers' Souk,
cajoling two camels and the small-hoofed donkey.
May we improvise mosaics in the maize and indigo plazas,
with our crazy families, over aqueducts made famous by warring
Romans, and through decaying archways,
followed by two camels and one disagreeable donkey.
May we jam in the amphitheater and read aloud our odes to friends
who will love and disappoint and delight us in the melodies of friendship,
remembering to water two camels and one obstinate donkey.
In blowing sand that stings our faces, with recollections of our dead tenderly
wrapped and shaped like pyramids, may we sway
rhythmically on the backs of two camels and one moody donkey.
May we cherish the desert and embrace our memories of the sea,
knowing that one does not cancel out the other
but permits a cobalt-blue feather to grow in the mind.
May we gather in temporary shelters and break bread with others,
never allowing our envy to get out of hand and respecting the laws
of the lands we cross on two camels and one petulant donkey.
Thus, the painter invented this fanciful checkerboard grid,
this landscape of magic squares into which we may walk
with our lives and our deaths, with two camels and one recalcitrant donkey.

playful,
but prayer-like

THE WILD HEART

Taught, like all Jewish kids, to curse a boast,
or any declaration of good luck, I refuse!
I bless the day we ran smack into
each other on Sixth Avenue. I'll let you
toi, toi, toi with my old bubbe. OK, I can't—
it's true—stop thinking I'll pay for this:
renounce the gods of joy, betray my principles, recant.
Oh darling, I'd like to surrender my one-
wrong-move philosophy, the slippery slope,
the fears of unwed motherhood, botulism,
poor expense records, impractical outer garments.
Today I put my faith in our natural gifts—
good humor, good friends, the nick-of-time—
in your wild heart that inclines toward mine.

Notes

"Head of an Angel": From the Dürer drawing with the same name.

"Manifest Destinies": In this found poem, I lineated sentences from *The Journals of Lewis and Clark*, edited by Bernard DeVoto (Boston: Houghton Mifflin Company, 1953).

"The Miniaturists": I am indebted to Willy Eisenhart for his discussion in *The World of Donald Evans* (New York: A Harlin Quist Book, 1980).

"Orienteer: The Childhood Drawings of William Steeple Davis, 1884–1961": William Steeple Davis, artist and photographer, lived and worked in Orient, New York.

"Soot and Spit": James Castle (1899–1977), outsider artist, lived and worked in Green Valley, Idaho.

"Head of an Old Man": From a drawing by Andrea del Sarto titled *Head of a Bald Old Man*.

"The Dome Fire": This fire swept northern New Mexico in May 1996.

"Angel Supporting St. Sebastian": From a drawing by Eustache Le Sueur with the same name.

"Qualities Boys Like Best in Girls": In this found poem, I juxtaposed and combined passages from *Guide for Today's Home Living*, by Mildred Andrews and Hazel Hatcher (Boston: D. C. Heath and Company, 1966).

"Simple Dark": From a drawing by Lambert Doomer titled *Village Street with a Barn*.

"With Two Camels and One Donkey": From a Paul Klee painting with the same name.

Acknowledgments

The author wishes to express her grateful acknowledgment to the following publications in which these poems, some in earlier versions, first appeared: *Alaska Quarterly Review* ("OK, Tucker"); *American Poetry Review* ("The Architect of Happiness," "Intersex," "The Miniaturists," "Old Dog," "Orienteer: The Childhood Drawings of William Steeple Davis, 1884–1961," and "Summer's Tale"); *Bloom* ("Salon"); *Cincinnati Review* ("Cohort"); *5AM* ("After the Snowstorm, the Bay" and "Lament of the Mangle"); *Forward* ("The New Egypt"); *Georgia Review* ("Against Pleasure" and "Sound View"); *New Letters* ("Borderline," "The Drawer," "Head of an Old Man" under the title "Head of a Bald Old Man," and "With Two Camels and One Donkey"); *Mid-American Review* ("Autumn Measure" and "Mah-Jongg Fantasia"); *Poetry* ("A Pasture of My Palm"); *Prairie Schooner* ("Holy Card," "On Friendship," "Soot and Spit," "Subject / Matter," and "The Wild Heart"); *Provincetown Arts* ("Angel Supporting St. Sebastian" under the title "Classical Lines"); *Rattapallax* ("Birds of Prey" under the title "Winter Pantoum," and "Description"); *River Oak Review* ("August," "The Dogs of Santorini," "Great Sleeps I Have Known," "Man of the Year," "Now," "The Outside Agitator," and "Rain"); *Women's Review of Books* ("Island of Daily Life" and "Late Butch-Femme").

"The Poconos" appears in *Common Wealth: Poets on Pennsylvania* (University Park: Pennsylvania State University Press, 2005).

"Against Pleasure" was reprinted in the December 2005 issue of *O: The Oprah Magazine.*

The following poems appear in *Venetian Blue*, a limited-edition chapbook published in 2002 by the Frick Art & Historical Center in Pittsburgh, Pennsylvania: "Head of an Angel" and "Simple Dark."

The last line of "Salon" and the title of this collection come from a sculpture and exhibition with the same name by artist Patricia Cronin.

I thank the English Department and the College of Liberal Arts of the Pennsylvania State University for a sabbatical that enabled me to complete this book. I am grateful to the trustees of the William Steeple Davis Foundation for a 2000-2001 residency during which I drafted many of these poems.

For assistance in the preparation of this manuscript, I thank Julie Abraham, James Brasfield, Lori Ginzberg, Miriam Goodman, Eloise Klein Healy, Charlotte Holmes, Susanna Kaysen, Maxine Kumin, Amy Lang, Leslie Lawrence, and Carolyn Sachs.